the no-potato passover

the
no-potato
passover

aviva kanoff

a journey of food, travel and color

The No-Potato Passover

International Standard Book Number: 0988910411
ISBN 13: 978-0-9889104-1-6

Printed in the United States of America

Edited: Rachel Honeyman
Book & Cover Design: Esther Rubin [design@estherrubin.com]
Photo Credits: Aviva Kanoff
              Dovid Gorman, p. 88

Recipe Credits: Elaine Birnbaum of Miami Beach
              Country Rustic Apple Pie (p. 153) & Chocolate Chip Biscotti (p. 159)

Thanks to the Ramat Family for the use of their Wagging Tail Farm

thank you

There are no words to express how grateful I am to my friends and family for their undying love, support, and encouragement throughout the production of this project. You all ate Passover food for an entire year until all my recipes were tested, re-tested and completed (not that you're complaining).

Special thanks to the following key players in this book production...

Rach, my incredible sister (in-law) who suggested I write this book in the first place

Rachel, my editor, for turning my doodles into coherent sentences

Arielle, for your brilliant recommendation

Esther G., you helped turn my dream into a reality

Stephen, for your gracious support and unending patience with all of my business endeavors

Dani Klein, for your consulting and web advertising

Daniella, my favorite foodie who's always up for brainstorming new recipe ideas

Frumie, for instilling in me a love of travel and culture

Michali and Chavie, my tenured and dear friends; your lifelong love and encouragement does not go unnoticed or unappreciated

Sara G.; your endless creativity, consistent brilliance, and constant enthusiasm. You define the word friendship

Dovid, for keeping me on the path to following my dreams. I don't know what I would do without your support and counsel

My incredible, devoted, and adoring parents; to thank you for all you have done would need its own book. I'm the luckiest girl in the world to have parents like you!

soups & salads

traditional chef salad 14
greek salad with mint & feta 15
golden ruby beet salad 16
guacamole..19
quinoa green salad 20
warm mushroom salad 21
grilled eggplant salad..23
heirloom tomato salad with honey basil vinaigrette ...24
lemon cucumber salad 25
poached peach & chicken salad 27
pomegranate & goat cheese salad...............................28
thai asian beef salad 31
roasted garlic soup with flanken 33
cream of broccoli soup with chives 35
cream of cauliflower soup 37
cabbage soup with matzo meatballs 38
roasted butternut squash soup 39

sides

garlic spaghetti squash with basil...............................42
salt & pepper kugel...43
quinoa & cabbage 44
cajun carrot fries...47
garlic brussels sprouts 48
tri-color cauliflower 51
sautéed greens with portabella mushrooms 53
cauliflower au gratin..55
mushroom spinach quinoa 56
rosemary butternut squash...57
mint & honey glazed baby carrots 58
roasted parsnips...59
stuffed zucchini blossoms 61
parsnip mash 63
spanish quinoa 65
ratatouille 67
mixed berry quinoa with roasted almonds 68
baby bok choy with garlic & ginger 69
quinoa taboule 71

meats

hungarian beef goulash 75
lamb shashlik 76
silver-tip roast with truffled mushroom sauce............77
pomegranate brisket 78
pistachio mint crusted rack of lamb 80
cranberry corned beef 81
sweet 'n' tangy brisket 82

beef & broccoli..83
meatballs & "spaghetti"..84
eggplant lasagna...87
southwestern sweet 'n' spicy meatballs....................89

poultry

strawberry glazed chicken 92
pesto chicken "pasta"...94
honey glazed turkey roast...95
lemon zested asparagus chicken...............................97
moroccan chicken..98
duck a l'orange..100
baked chicken with fennel & carrots.......................101
jamaican jerk chicken 103
coq au vin with saffron quinoa 104
citrus chicken 107
coconut crusted chicken with plum dipping sauce ..109
honey mustard schnitzel...110
grilled chicken with spicy mango salsa 113
lavender mint roasted chicken 114
chicken w. apricot marmalade, balsamic vinaigrette116
mediterranean chicken 117

dairy & pareve entrées

"pasta" primavera..120
baked "ziti" 123
mint & honey baked salmon....................................124
salmon croquettes with wild mushroom sauce 127
moroccan baked salmon 128
rosemary walnut crusted salmon with garlic aioli 131
tuscan tuna steak with mint yogurt sauce.................132
honey mustard poached salmon 135
fresh sea bass with grapefruit relish.........................136
eggplant parmigiana 138

desserts

carrot muffins 142
apple cranberry crunch 145
banana cake...146
viennese crunch 149
coconut cream pie in a macaroon crust...................150
raspberry shortcake trifle 151
country rustic apple pie 153
blueberry crumble..154
hazelnut cream cookies..156
no-bake chocolate mousse pie 157
chocolate chip biscotti 159
kids' favorite chocolate chip cupcakes....................160

81

113

131

138

154

foreword

"Passover without potatoes? Impossible! We'll starve!"—This is the typical reaction I hear whenever I tell people about The No-Potato Passover. If you had the same reaction when you first saw the title of this book, let me tell you, the LAST thing you'll do is starve!

So how did this crazy idea come about?

I've always loved to experiment when it comes to cooking, creating recipes as colorful and interesting as possible. I've worked as a personal chef for several years, and I've noticed that many people fall into a cooking rut making the same three or four dishes again and again. They may have been great dishes to start, but after a while they become the same old, repetitive meals you always make.

This cooking rut is even more pronounced on Passover, having to cook twenty-four meals when food options are limited and we end up turning to good ol' potatoes as our Passover staple. Well, I wrote this cookbook to change the way we think about Passover food, and to put an end to the cooking rut.

A couple of years ago, as Passover was fast approaching, just as I found myself dreading the very thought of another potato-filled Passover, someone proposed a fantastic idea

to me: creating a low-carb Passover cookbook. Since I love a good challenge more than anything, I dove right in! At first, I was a bit apprehensive, but I decided to view this as an opportunity to use my innate creativity to help people find some interesting new recipes—while eliminating a Passover staple. The result of this challenge? Not only have I forced myself to experiment, but I also now find potatoes to be the blandest of foods—obviously excluding the occasional French fry!

Does this mean I'll never cook another potato? Of course not! I just wanted to cut out potatoes for the purpose of this challenge to force myself to think outside the box and come up with lots of potato alternatives.

Trust me, the last thing I want is for you to feel limited by the lack of potatoes, but for the purpose of this challenge, I did not use either white or sweet potatoes in any recipe—even though I generally encourage people to use sweet potatoes all the time in their cooking, as it is one of the most nutritious root vegetables. Feel free to incorporate potatoes into any of the recipes in this book, but do me—and yourself!—a favor and try the original recipe first.

You might be surprised!

This is not just a cookbook; it is also an expression of my artistic sensibilities. I am an explorer by nature, and I have a natural curiosity to wonder what else is "out there." This curiosity has sent me around the world on a mission to find out what other countries and cultures look like, what they eat, how they dress, and how they live. You'll find many photographs from my travels throughout this book.

As a visual artist I am drawn to vibrant colors, so you will find many colorful recipes in this book. Maybe that's why I'm not as fascinated by white potatoes as I am by rainbow chard or golden beets. Either way, by cutting out potatoes and substituting other vegetables, you not only experience a variety of flavors, but many vital nutrients as well. Generally, the more naturally colorful the food, the more nutrients and vitamins it contains.

Lots of colorful travel photography has been included to satisfy the visual needs of the cook. The recipes I am usually drawn to are the ones that include pictures of the places to which the food is native. Hopefully, this book will be creatively challenging, exciting, indulging and satisfying to the cook with a touch of wanderlust. If you are stuck in the kitchen, you can at least daydream!

But in regards to being trapped in the kitchen, I haven't included any time consuming recipes. Passover is about being free from slavery; being enslaved in the kitchen would not be in the spirit of the holiday.

Enjoy!

Aviva

"What are we gonna eat, if not potatoes?!"

Allow me to introduce two important super foods in this book. Both packed with nutrition, low in calories and carbohydrates, and easily disguised to produce an abundance of flavors!

Spaghetti Squash

Okay, so it doesn't taste exactly like the real thing, but it's pretty close, and the calorie count is well worth it! (One cup serving of cooked spaghetti squash has 42 calories vs. 1 cup of cooked pasta, which has 221 calories.) Additionally, because spaghetti squash is a vegetable, it's much lower in carbohydrates and won't leave you feeling lethargic.

One cup of cooked pasta contains 42 grams of carbohydrates, while one cup of spaghetti squash contains 10 grams of carbohydrates.

Quinoa

Most commonly considered a grain, quinoa is actually a chenopad, a relative of leafy green vegetables like spinach and Swiss chard. Rich in amino acids, it is a recently rediscovered ancient "grain" once considered "the gold of the Incas." While technically it is a seed, it is not considered to be kitniyot by most rabbinic authorities and is permissible to be eaten on Passover.
(Check with your local rabbi.)

fresh tomato basil sauce

INGREDIENTS

- 2 lbs. very ripe tomatoes, diced
- 5 cloves garlic, chopped
- ¼ cup olive oil
- 10 basil leaves
- 1 large Vidalia onion, diced

This homemade tomato sauce is delicious in the Baked Ziti (p. 123) and Eggplant Parmigiana (p. 138)!

DIRECTIONS

1. Heat oil in large pot.
2. Sauté onion and garlic until browned.
3. Add tomatoes and basil leaves.
4. Cook for 30 minutes on medium flame.

walnut pesto

INGREDIENTS

- 2 cups fresh basil leaves
- 2 cups walnuts
- 5 cloves garlic
- 1 cup olive oil
- salt and pepper to taste
- for dairy, add ½ cup Parmesan cheese

This walnut pesto is perfect in the Pesto Chicken Pasta on page 94!

DIRECTIONS

1. Blend all ingredients in blender or food processor until finely ground.

soups
& salads

traditional chef salad

INGREDIENTS

- 3 hearts green and red romaine lettuces
- 1 red onion, thinly sliced
- 2 cups grape tomatoes, halved
- 3 assorted bell peppers, thinly sliced
- 1 large cucumber, diced
- 1 avocado, diced

Dressing:
- ¼ cup sugar
- ¾ cup mayonnaise
- 5 tbsp. imitation honey mustard
- 2 tbsp. lemon juice
- 3 tbsp. olive oil
- 1 tbsp. chopped parsley

DIRECTIONS

1. Chop and combine all vegetables in a large bowl.
2. Mix dressing, pour over vegetables, and toss.
3. Cut up some cold deli meat, leftover turkey, or corned beef into cubes, and sprinkle over the top of the salad.

greek salad with mint & feta

INGREDIENTS

- 1½ lbs. tomatoes, cored and diced (4 cups)
- 2 tbsp. torn mint leaves
- 2 radishes, thinly sliced
- ¼ cup extra virgin olive oil
- salt and pepper

- 2 cups baby arugula
- ½ cup crumbled feta cheese
- 1 tsp. lime or lemon juice

DIRECTIONS

1. In a bowl, toss the tomatoes with mint, radishes and olive oil.
2. Season with salt and pepper.
3. Add the arugula and most of the feta, and toss gently.
4. Transfer the salad to a platter and sprinkle remaining feta on top, then squeeze or pour lime/lemon juice over the top of the salad.

golden ruby beet salad

INGREDIENTS

- 6 beets (3 gold, 3 red), diced
- 2 green onions, chopped
- 2 tbsp. cilantro, finely chopped
- 1 tbsp. olive oil
- ¼ cup balsamic vinegar
- ¼ cup maple syrup or honey
- juice of 1 lime
- 1 tsp. cumin

DIRECTIONS

1. Boil beets in water for an hour, until soft.
2. Cool beets, then peel and dice.
3. Chop onions and cilantro, and add to diced beets.
4. In a separate bowl, mix together olive oil, balsamic vinegar, maple syrup, lime juice, and cumin.
5. Pour over beets, onions, and cilantro.
6. Serve chilled.

HAVANA 1957

CUBAN CUSINE

Tapas & Tinto

guacamole

INGREDIENTS

- 4 avocados
- 2 tbsp. lemon juice
- 3 scallions, chopped
- salt and pepper
- garlic powder

DIRECTIONS

1. Peel and mash avocados.
2. Mix with lemon juice and spices.
3. Serve and enjoy.

Guacamole can be used as a wonderful dip for matzo! For a low-carb option, serve with carrot sticks.

Spice up your holiday and have a Mexican fiesta themed meal combining guacamole with Spanish quinoa (p. 65) and grilled chicken with mango salsa (p. 113)!

quinoa green salad

INGREDIENTS

- 4 cups mixed salad greens
- 1 cup purple cabbage, thinly sliced
- 1 cup grape or cherry tomatoes, halved
- ½ cup green onions, diagonally cut
- ½ cup quinoa, cooked
- 1 cup carrots, shredded
- 2 avocados, diced

Dressing:
- 3 tbsp. balsamic vinegar
- 1 tbsp. fresh lemon juice
- 1 tbsp. imitation mustard
- 1 tsp. fresh dill, chopped
- 3 tsp. olive oil
- 1 tsp. honey
- ¼ tsp. freshly ground black pepper
- ⅛ tsp. salt

DIRECTIONS

1. Combine salad ingredients in a large bowl.
2. In a small bowl, mix dressing ingredients.
3. Pour dressing over the salad. Mix and serve.

warm mushroom salad

INGREDIENTS

- 3½ tbsp. olive oil
- 1½ cups fresh mushrooms, sliced
- 1 clove garlic, chopped (optional)
- 2½ tbsp. balsamic vinegar
- 1 tsp. honey
- salt and pepper to taste
- 1 (10 oz.) package baby greens
- ½ cup sun-dried tomatoes
- ½ cup hearts of palm, sliced
- handful of almonds, slivered

DIRECTIONS

1. Heat 1 tbsp. of olive oil in a skillet over medium heat. Add mushrooms, stirring until soft. Continue cooking until the juices from the mushrooms have reduced to about 2 tbsp.
2. Stir in the remaining olive oil, balsamic vinegar, salt and pepper until evenly blended. Turn off heat, and let the mushrooms sit in the pan until they are just warm, but no longer hot—otherwise the greens will wilt too much.
3. Put the baby greens into a serving bowl, and pour the warm mushroom mixture over them.
4. Toss to blend, and serve immediately.

grilled eggplant salad

INGREDIENTS

- 1 large eggplant
- 3 large tomatoes
- 1 red pepper
- 1 large onion, diced
- 5 cloves garlic, whole

- 3 tbsp. olive oil
- salt and pepper to taste
- 1 tsp. cumin
- 1 tsp. lemon juice
- 1 tsp. balsamic vinegar
- 1 tsp. sugar

DIRECTIONS

1. Preheat oven to 400°.
2. Slice eggplant, tomatoes, pepper, and garlic into ¼-inch chunks.
3. Drizzle with olive oil and roast for 20 minutes, or until browned.
4. Sauté diced onion in olive oil.
5. Add roasted vegetables and cook until veggies blend together to create a sauce-like consistency.
6. Flavor with lemon juice, vinegar, sugar, cumin, salt and pepper.

heirloom tomato salad with honey basil vinaigrette

INGREDIENTS

- heirloom tomatoes
- mixed greens

Dressing:
- ¼ cup honey
- ½ cup olive oil
- ¼ cup balsamic vinegar
- 1 clove garlic
- ½ cup fresh basil
- dash of salt

DIRECTIONS

1. Slice tomatoes and spread over a bed of greens.
2. Mix dressing ingredients in a blender.
3. Pour dressing over sliced heirloom tomatoes and greens, and serve.

Tip: Dressing can be stored in the refrigerator for up to one week.

lemon cucumber salad

INGREDIENTS

- 4 cucumbers, thinly sliced
- 1 small white onion, thinly sliced
- 1 tsp. lemon juice
- 1 cup white vinegar
- ½ cup water
- ¾ cup white sugar
- 1 tbsp. dried or fresh dill

DIRECTIONS

1. Toss together the cucumbers and onion in a large bowl.
2. Combine the vinegar, water, and sugar in a saucepan over medium-high heat. Bring to a boil, and pour over the cucumber and onions.
3. Stir in dill, cover, and refrigerate until cold. This salad can also be eaten at room temperature, but be sure to allow the cucumbers to marinate for at least 1 hour.

Tip: Substitute chicken with $\frac{1}{4}$ cup feta cheese for a dairy meal.

poached peach & chicken salad

INGREDIENTS

- ¾ cup balsamic vinegar
- 2 sprigs fresh thyme
- Kosher salt & ground black pepper
- 2 peaches
  (12 oz. total), halved & pitted
- 4½ tsp. olive oil
- 4 cups baby greens

Chicken:
- 1 lb. chicken breasts
- 1 tsp. salt
- 1½ tsp. paprika
- ⅛ tsp. garlic powder
- ⅛ tsp. onion powder
- 2 tbsp. honey
- 2 tbsp. olive oil
- 2 tsp. cumin
- 2 tsp. rosemary
- salt & pepper

DIRECTIONS

1. Prepare a medium gas or charcoal grill fire. (Note: If you don't have a grill, you can cook the chicken in a sauté pan in its marinade.)
2. Combine vinegar and thyme in a 2-quart saucepan. Bring to a boil over medium heat.
3. Reduce the heat to a simmer and cook until the mixture is thick, syrupy, and reduced to ¼ cup, about 6-9 minutes.
4. Cook peaches in the syrup for 2 minutes until soft. Remove from the heat, discard the thyme sprigs, and season with a pinch of salt and a few grinds of black pepper.
5. Season chicken and grill or sauté in a pan until cooked.
6. In a medium bowl, toss the baby greens with the remaining 2½ tsp. oil and season to taste with salt and pepper. Arrange on a platter.
7. Top with the chicken and peaches. Drizzle with about 2 tbsp. of the reduced balsamic, adding more to taste. Season to taste with salt, pepper, and remaining juice from chicken and peaches.

pomegranate & goat cheese salad

INGREDIENTS

- 1 tbsp. olive oil
- 1 tbsp. sugar
- ½ tsp. salt
- 8 cups mixed baby greens
- ¼ cup pomegranate seeds
- 4 tbsp. crumbled goat cheese (or feta)

Dressing:
- 2 tbsp. balsamic vinegar
- 2 tbsp. extra virgin olive oil
- 3 tbsp. maple syrup

DIRECTIONS

1. Toss greens, pomegranate seeds, and goat cheese in a large bowl.
2. Whisk together vinegar, olive oil and maple syrup in a small bowl and drizzle over tossed salad. Serve immediately.

Ardith Mae
FARMSTEAD GOAT CHEESE

Fresh Chevre $8
- Lightly Salted w/sea salt

Garic Scape + Black Pepper Chevre $9

Herb Chevre $6
- fresh Chev coated in herbs

FETA
Brine

thai asian beef salad

INGREDIENTS

- 3 heads green and red romaine lettuces
- 1 red onion, thinly sliced
- 2 cups grape tomatoes, halved
- 3 assorted bell peppers, thinly sliced
- 1 lb. London broil
- ½ cup imitation soy sauce

Dressing:
- ¾ cup sugar
- ¾ cup olive oil
- ⅓ cup white vinegar
- 2 tsp. imitation soy sauce

DIRECTIONS

1. Marinate meat in soy sauce.
2. Broil the meat for 10 minutes.
3. Slice the meat after it has cooled for 30 minutes.
4. Toss meat with salad and serve.

Tip: Flanken can be set aside and served separately, if desired.

roasted garlic soup with flanken

INGREDIENTS

- 40 garlic cloves, unpeeled
- 4 tbsp. olive oil
- 1 piece of flanken with bone
- 2¼ cups sliced onions
- 1½ tsp. fresh thyme, chopped
- 3½ cups chicken stock or canned low-salt chicken broth

DIRECTIONS

1. Preheat oven to 350°.
2. Place 40 unpeeled garlic cloves in a small glass baking dish. Add 2 tbsp. olive oil and sprinkle with salt and pepper. Toss to coat.
3. Cover baking dish tightly with foil and bake until garlic is golden brown and tender, about 45 minutes.
4. Remove garlic from oven and let it cool. Then squeeze garlic between fingertips to release cloves from peel. Transfer to a small bowl.
5. Heat remaining oil in a large saucepan over medium-high heat. Add onions and thyme, and cook until onions are translucent, about 6 minutes.
6. Add roasted garlic and cook for 3 minutes.
7. Add flanken and brown for 2 minutes.
8. Add chicken stock. Cover and simmer until garlic is very tender, about 20 minutes.
9. Remove flanken and discard.
10. Purée soup with a hand mixer or blender until smooth.

Tip: Use these beautiful flowering chives as a garnish!

cream of broccoli soup with chives

INGREDIENTS

- 1 large onion, diced
- 3 large garlic cloves, sliced thinly
- 2 tbsp. canola oil
- 2 lbs. frozen or fresh broccoli florets
- 8 cups chicken stock

- 2 cups almond milk
- ¼ cup white cooking wine
- 1 tsp. salt
- 1 tbsp. lemon juice
- 1 handful of chopped chives to garnish

DIRECTIONS

1. Heat the oil in a large stockpot over medium heat. Add onion and garlic and sauté gently until softened and translucent, about 3 minutes.
2. Add broccoli and chicken stock and bring to a boil. Reduce heat, then cover and simmer for 20 minutes. Add salt, lemon juice, and white wine.
3. Let the soup cool a bit, then put soup in blender until smooth. This will have to be done in batches.
4. Return soup to pot through a strainer. Not all of the contents will make it through the strainer.
5. Reserve the thick parts that won't strain and put them back into the blender, then pour back into the soup.
6. Reheat the soup on medium heat. Add almond milk and stir. Add more salt and pepper to taste.
7. Before serving, garnish with chives.

cream of cauliflower soup

INGREDIENTS

- 1 head cauliflower, separated into pieces
- 1 tbsp. olive oil
- garlic powder
- 1 red pepper, diced
- 1 yellow pepper, diced
- 4 white mushrooms, diced
- 1 large onion, diced
- 8 cups chicken broth
- 2 cups almond milk
- 2 tbsp. mayonnaise
- 1 tbsp. matzo meal (optional)

DIRECTIONS

1. Preheat oven to 400°.
2. Sauté onions, mushrooms, and peppers until soft.
3. Roast cauliflower sprinkled with olive oil and garlic in oven for 40 minutes.
4. When all vegetables are cooked, combine all vegetables in a stockpot along with chicken broth, almond milk, mayonnaise, and matzo meal.
5. Bring soup to a boil and cook for 30 minutes.
6. Shut off flame and allow soup to cool, then blend in food processor, blender, or with a hand mixer.

cabbage soup with matzo meatballs

INGREDIENTS

- 1 large onion, diced
- 4 garlic cloves, chopped
- 5 tbsp. canola oil
- 1 tbsp. sugar
- 4 tomatoes, diced

- 1 large green cabbage, chopped
- 8 cups chicken stock
- 1 tbsp. honey
- 2 cups tomato sauce

Matzo Meatballs:
- ½ cup matzo meal
- ½ lb. ground beef
- 3 eggs
- salt and pepper
- 1 tbsp. oregano
- 1 tsp. cumin

DIRECTIONS

1. Sauté onion and garlic in canola oil until brown.
2. Add sugar and caramelize.
3. Add remaining ingredients and bring to a boil.
4. Let boil for 30 minutes and then simmer.
5. While the soup is boiling, mix all ingredients for the matzo meatballs.
6. Form into balls, then add the matzo meatballs to the boiling soup. Cook for 20 minutes.

roasted butternut squash soup

INGREDIENTS

- 1 small butternut squash (about 1 lb.), quartered lengthwise
- 4-6 garlic cloves, peeled and chopped
- 3 tbsp. olive oil
- 1 medium onion, peeled and finely chopped
- 2 celery stalks, finely sliced
- 1 carrot, finely sliced
- 1 turnip, finely sliced
- 8-12 cups chicken stock (fresh or from consommé)
- salt and freshly ground pepper
- 1 tbsp. cumin

DIRECTIONS

1. Preheat oven to 350°.
2. Place the butternut squash on a baking tray.
3. Brush the surface of the squash with olive oil and season it with salt and pepper.
4. Bake for 25 minutes. Add the garlic and continue baking for another 15 minutes or until soft.
5. Remove the squash from the oven and let it cool completely, then scoop out the flesh and discard the skin.
6. While the squash is cooling, heat the oil in a large pot. Add the onion, celery, carrot, and garlic, and cook on low heat for 10 minutes until soft, but not brown.
7. Pour the chicken stock over the vegetables, and bring to a boil.
8. Simmer vegetables for 5-10 minutes.
9. Add the butternut squash (scooped out of the skin) and continue cooking for another 5 minutes, then remove the soup from the heat.
10. Allow soup to cool, then blend the soup with a hand blender or in a food processor. Check for seasoning and serve.

sides

garlic spaghetti squash with basil

INGREDIENTS

- 2 cups spaghetti squash, baked, seeded, and shredded
- 5 garlic cloves, chopped
- 1 cup grape tomatoes, halved
- 10 basil leaves
- 1 large onion, sliced into rings
- 5 tbsp. olive oil
- salt and pepper

DIRECTIONS

1. Sauté onions and garlic until brown.
2. Add spaghetti squash, tomatoes, basil, salt and pepper.
3. Mix for 2 minutes, then serve warm.

salt & pepper kugel

INGREDIENTS

- 3 cups spaghetti squash, shredded
- 3 large eggs
- 1 tsp. salt
- 1 tsp. pepper
- 2 tsp. sugar
- ¼ cup matzo meal
- ¼ cup canola oil

DIRECTIONS

1. Preheat oven to 350°.
2. Mix all ingredients except for the oil.
3. Pour oil into a 9×12-inch pan, and place in preheated oven for 5 minutes.
4. Pour squash mixture into hot oil.
5. Bake for 45 minutes.
6. Remove kugel from oven and pour off excess oil.
7. If the kugel is still too watery, bake out some of the moisture before serving.

quinoa & cabbage

INGREDIENTS

- 1 cup quinoa, cooked according to package
- 3 cups green cabbage, shredded
- 1 large onion, diced
- vegetable oil for sauté
- 3 tbsp. sugar
- salt and pepper to taste

DIRECTIONS

1. Brown the onion and caramelize in oil and sugar.
2. Add cabbage and sauté until cooked, about 5 minutes.
3. Reduce the fire and add cooked quinoa, stirring for about 2 minutes.
4. Simmer and add salt and pepper to taste. You can add more sugar for a sweeter variation.

cajun carrot fries

INGREDIENTS

- 8-10 large carrots, peeled and cut into thin slices, like "fries"
- 1 tbsp. olive oil
- ¼ tsp. cayenne pepper
- salt and black pepper to taste

DIRECTIONS

1. Preheat oven to 450°.
2. Grease and/or line a large cookie sheet.
3. Toss the sliced carrots with olive oil, cayenne pepper, salt and black pepper.
4. Arrange the fries in a single layer on your baking sheet and bake for 15 minutes, then flip the fries over and bake for another 10-15 minutes, until crisp. Serve warm.

garlic brussels sprouts

INGREDIENTS

- 16 oz. Brussels sprouts, cut in half
- 5 tbsp. olive oil
- garlic powder
- salt and pepper

DIRECTIONS

1. Preheat oven to 400°.
2. Rub olive oil, generous amount of garlic powder, salt and pepper on Brussels sprouts.
3. Pour Brussels sprout mixture into a 9×12-inch pan.
4. Roast uncovered, for 45 minutes or until golden.

tri-color cauliflower

INGREDIENTS

- 1 head purple cauliflower
- 1 head orange cauliflower
- 1 head green cauliflower
- 4 garlic cloves
- olive oil
- salt and pepper

DIRECTIONS

1. Preheat oven to 450°.
2. Clean and chop the cauliflower into bite-sized pieces.
3. Mince 4 garlic cloves.
4. In a bowl, combine the cauliflower, garlic, 2 tsp. kosher salt, and fresh ground pepper. Add just enough olive oil to lightly coat the cauliflower and toss.
5. Spread the cauliflower on a baking sheet and bake for around 40 minutes or until browned, turning once.

Tip: While tri-color cauliflower is fun and festive when available, don't worry if you can only find good ol' plain white. It tastes just as delicious!

sautéed greens with portabella mushrooms

INGREDIENTS

- 3 garlic cloves, whole
- 1 bag fresh spinach
- 1 bushel Swiss chard, tops and bottoms trimmed
- 3 portabella mushrooms

DIRECTIONS

1. Sauté garlic until brown.
2. Add sliced portabella mushrooms, spinach, and Swiss chard.
3. Sauté all together for about 2 minutes until spinach and Swiss chard are soft but not too wilted.
4. Add salt and pepper to taste.

ST. TROPEZ, FRANCE

cauliflower au gratin

INGREDIENTS

- 6 tbsp. margarine
- ½ cup matzo cake meal or ground walnuts
- 2 large onions, chopped
- ½ cup mayonnaise
- ½ tsp. salt

- 28 oz. chicken stock
- 1 large cauliflower, sliced into ¼-inch slices
- black pepper
- paprika

DIRECTIONS

1. Preheat oven to 350°.
2. In a large pot, melt margarine.
3. Add matzo meal or ground walnuts and whisk until smooth.
4. Add onions, mayonnaise, salt, and chicken stock. Stir until smooth and cook until broth thickens.
5. With ladle, spread a layer of sauce at the bottom of a 9×13-inch greased pan. Spread a layer of cauliflower. Repeat to form a layered effect.
6. Sprinkle with paprika and pepper.
7. Bake for 1½ hours, or until golden brown.

mushroom spinach quinoa

INGREDIENTS

- 2 cups fresh spinach, chopped
- 1 cup quinoa
- 2 cups mushrooms, diced
- 1 large onion, diced
- salt, pepper and garlic powder to season

DIRECTIONS

1. Cook quinoa according to package and set aside.
2. In a large frying pan, brown onions.
3. Add mushrooms and spinach.
4. Sauté for 3 minutes until fully cooked.
5. Mix quinoa together with spinach, mushrooms and onions.
6. Season with salt, pepper and garlic.

rosemary butternut squash

INGREDIENTS

- 1 large butternut squash, peeled, seeded and cubed
- 3 tbsp. olive oil
- 1 tsp. rosemary
- salt and pepper

DIRECTIONS

1. Mix all ingredients together and spread in a greased 9×12-inch pan.
2. Bake uncovered at 400° for 40 minutes or until roasted.

mint & honey glazed baby carrots

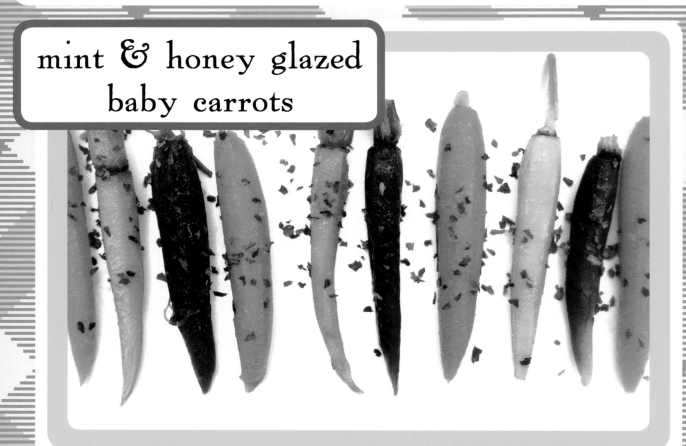

INGREDIENTS

- 16 oz. baby carrots
- 1 tbsp. canola oil
- ½ tsp. chopped mint
- 1 tbsp. honey

Tip: A little mint goes a long way. Don't use too much or your carrots may taste a bit too much like toothpaste!

DIRECTIONS

1. Boil carrots in water until soft, about 30 minutes, then strain them.
2. Heat oil in a pan.
3. Sauté carrots in oil, then add honey and mint.
4. Stir for 2 minutes until carrots are fully glazed.

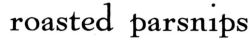

roasted parsnips

INGREDIENTS

- ⅓ cup olive oil
- 3 medium parsnips (about 1 lb.), cut into 1½-inch thick slices
- 1 tbsp. dried oregano
- 1 tbsp. dried rosemary
- 1 tbsp. dried thyme
- 1 tbsp. dried basil
- 1½ tsp. sea salt
- 2 tsp. freshly ground black pepper

DIRECTIONS

1. Preheat oven to 400° and lightly coat an 11×17-inch baking sheet with olive oil.
2. In a large bowl, combine all ingredients and toss to coat. Spread evenly on a prepared baking sheet. Add more olive oil if the vegetables seem dry.
3. Place in preheated oven and bake for 35-40 minutes.

stuffed zucchini blossoms

INGREDIENTS

- 6-10 zucchini blossoms, pistils removed
- 6 mushrooms, diced
- 1 large onion, diced
- 1 cup spinach
- 1 cup ricotta cheese
- salt and pepper to taste
- oil for frying

DIRECTIONS

1. Carefully rinse the zucchini blossoms and remove the pistils.
2. Heat 1 inch of oil in a frying pan over medium-high heat.
3. Sauté onions and spinach until soft.
4. Add ricotta cheese to onion and spinach, and mix for 2 minutes.
5. Fill each blossom with cheese and spinach mixture. Repeat until all blossoms are stuffed.
6. Heat additional oil in frying pan.
7. Carefully place each stuffed blossom in the oil. (Note: Fry in batches if you need to; don't overcrowd the pan.)
8. Fry until browned, about 3-4 minutes, turning occasionally.
9. Transfer to a paper towel lined plate with a slotted spoon. Sprinkle with more kosher salt if desired. Serve hot.

DORSET, ENGLAND

parsnip mash

INGREDIENTS

- 6 medium parsnips
- 1 large onion, diced
- 6 mushrooms, diced
- 5 tbsp. canola oil
- 1 tbsp. butter or margarine

Tip: Cheat if you must and substitute some of the parsnips with potatoes.

DIRECTIONS

1. Boil parsnips in water until soft.
2. Sauté onions and mushrooms in canola oil until brown, and then set aside.
3. Strain parsnips and place in mixing bowl.
4. Mash parsnips and add butter, mushroom, and onions.
5. Season with salt and pepper to taste.

spanish quinoa

INGREDIENTS

- 1 cup quinoa, cooked according to package
- 1 red bell pepper, diced
- 1 yellow bell pepper, diced
- 1 orange bell pepper, diced
- 1 large onion, chopped
- 1 lb ground beef (optional)
- salt, pepper, and garlic powder to season

DIRECTIONS

1. Sauté onion until brown.
2. Add peppers and ground beef until cooked, about 5 minutes. (Peppers should be soft and beef should be brown.)
3. Turn off flame and season with salt, pepper and garlic powder.
4. Combine pepper and beef mixture with cooked quinoa, and serve warm.

GIVERNY, FRANCE

ratatouille

INGREDIENTS

- 2 Japanese eggplants, sliced into ¼-inch circles
- 5-6 campari tomatoes, sliced ¼-inch circles
- 4 zucchinis, sliced ¼-inch circles
- fresh garlic, minced
- ¼ cup olive oil
- 1 cup tomato sauce
- Herbes de Provence (oregano, basil, thyme, parsley)
- salt and pepper

DIRECTIONS

1. Preheat oven to 350°.
2. Spray a 9×12-inch baking dish with cooking spray.
3. Layer tomatoes and drizzle with olive oil and herbs.
4. Repeat with eggplant and then zucchini.
5. Cover with tomato sauce.
6. Cover and bake for 45 minutes.
7. When fully baked, pour out excess liquid.

mixed berry quinoa with roasted almonds

INGREDIENTS

- 1 cup red quinoa
- 1 cup slivered almonds
- 1 cup white quinoa
- 5-6 medium mushrooms, chopped
- 1 cup golden raisins
- 1 Vidalia onion, diced
- 1 cup craisins
- 2 tbsp. canola oil
- salt and pepper to taste

DIRECTIONS

1. Cook quinoa according to package.
2. In a separate skillet, sauté onions in canola oil until golden brown.
3. Add chopped mushrooms and sauté for one minute.
4. Add raisins, craisins and almonds, and sauté for another minute.
5. When quinoa is ready, add to pan and mix with other ingredients.
6. Add salt and pepper to taste.

baby bok choy with garlic & ginger

INGREDIENTS

- 3 heads of baby bok choy, trim the greens, chop and rinse in a bowl of water
- 1 tsp. ground or fresh ginger (you can add more if desired)
- 3 tbsp. olive oil
- 3 tbsp. imitation soy sauce
- 2 large garlic cloves, thinly sliced

DIRECTIONS

1. Trim greens from baby bok choy, then chop, and rinse in a bowl of water.
2. Heat the olive oil in a skillet on medium heat. Add the ginger and garlic, and stir to avoid sticking for about 2 minutes.
3. Add the bok choy and soy sauce, then sauté until tender but still al dente. Remove from heat.

ISRAEL

quinoa taboule

INGREDIENTS

- 1 cup quinoa
- 2 cups vegetable broth
- 2 cups Italian parsley
- 2 tomatoes, chopped
- 1 pepper, chopped
- 1 cucumber, chopped
- 2 green onions, chopped
- 1 small red onion, chopped
- 1 garlic clove, minced
- juice of 1-2 lemons, depending on your preference
- 2 tbsp. extra virgin olive oil
- salt and pepper to taste
- 1 tsp. cumin (optional)

DIRECTIONS

1. Bring the vegetable broth to a boil. Once boiling, pour in the cup of quinoa and simmer for 20 minutes on stovetop.
2. While quinoa is simmering, chop all of the vegetables.
3. After 20 minutes of simmering, drain the quinoa and combine it with the vegetables in a large bowl.
4. Pour lemon juice, olive oil, and seasoning over quinoa and vegetables. Mix well.

meats

BUDAPEST, HUNGARY

hungarian beef goulash

INGREDIENTS

- 2 lbs. beef chuck, cut into thin strips
- 1 large onion, sliced into rings
- 2 tbsp. oil
- 1 bay leaf
- 2 garlic cloves, whole
- 1 tsp. salt
- ½ tsp. pepper
- 1 tsp. paprika
- 1½ cups beef stock

DIRECTIONS

1. Heat oil in a skillet, then brown beef on both sides.
2. Add onion, stirring until onions are tender.
3. Add remaining ingredients and bring to a boil.
4. Cover and simmer on low heat for 1 hour. Stir frequently to keep from burning bottom of pan. Add more water, if necessary.

lamb shashlik

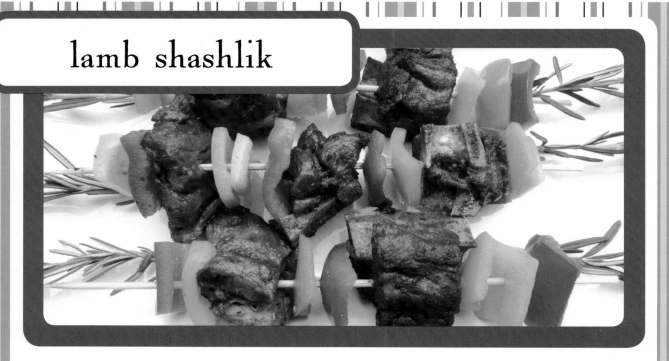

INGREDIENTS

- 1 lb. lamb trimmed of all fat, and cut into 2-inch cubes (leg or shoulder of lamb)
- ½ cup lemon juice
- ¼ cup garlic, chopped
- ½ cup olive oil
- 1 tsp. black pepper
- 1 tsp. salt
- 1 tbsp. rosemary
- 2 medium onions, cut into eighths
- 2 large peppers (of assorted colors), cut into 1-inch chunks

Note: The meat and veggies are cooked on different skewers because the meat will take longer to grill.

DIRECTIONS

1. In a bowl, combine lamb, lemon juice, garlic, olive oil, pepper, salt, and rosemary.
2. Marinate for at least 2-3 hours prior to cooking.
3. Place marinated beef on skewers (about 6 cubes per skewer).
4. Be sure to apply a light coat of oil on the skewer prior to threading the meat.
5. Place onion and pepper on separate skewers, alternating type of vegetable.
6. Cook lamb shashlik skewers on grill or under broiler for 10-12 minutes, or until desired doneness. Turn to ensure even cooking.
7. Grill vegetable skewers for last 5 minutes of grilling. Turn. The vegetables should be crisp, yet tender. Be careful not to overcook.

silver tip roast with truffled mushroom sauce

INGREDIENTS

- 5-lb. silver tip roast
- 1 large onion, diced
- ¼ tsp. salt
- ¼ tsp. pepper
- 1 tbsp. paprika
- 1 tbsp. garlic powder or fresh garlic, chopped
- 1 tbsp. olive oil

Mushroom Sauce:
- 10 assorted mushrooms, sliced thinly
- ¼ cup white wine
- 5 tbsp. almond milk
- 2 tbsp. olive oil
- 1 tbsp. truffle oil (if available)
- 1 tbsp. parsley, chopped (fresh or flakes)

DIRECTIONS

1. Preheat oven to 400°.
2. Spread diced onion in a large roasting pan, then place the roast on top of the onion.
3. Rub roast with paprika, salt, pepper, garlic, and olive oil.
4. Cover and place in oven for 1½-2 hours.
5. While the roast is in the oven, put mushrooms, wine, almond milk, and oil in
6. a sauté pan, and cook for 5 minutes. Then season with salt, pepper, and parsley.
7. When the roast is done, pour mushroom sauce on top of the roast and let sit for
8. at least 15 minutes before serving.

pomegranate brisket

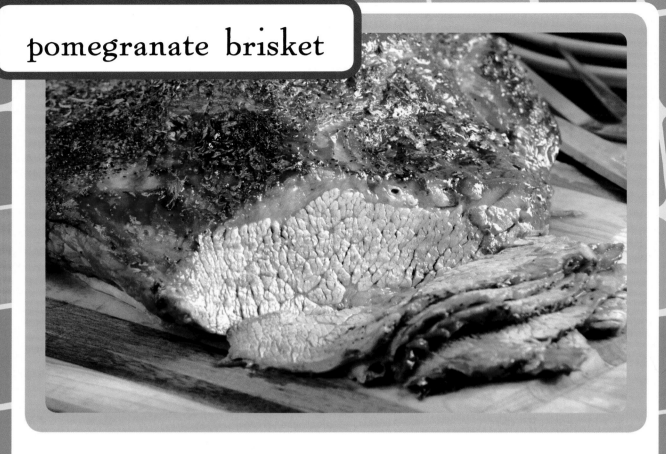

INGREDIENTS

- 5-lb. brisket
- ½ cup red wine
- ½ cup pomegranate juice
  (you can use Ceres brand youngberry juice
  if pomegranate is unavailable)
- 3 tbsp. honey
- 3 tbsp. imitation mustard

- 5 tbsp. olive oil
- 1 tbsp. rosemary
- salt and pepper
- paprika
- 1 large beet, diced
- ½ cup pomegranate seeds
  (optional)
- 1 large onion, diced

DIRECTIONS

1. Preheat oven to 400°.
2. Place roast in an extra large roasting pan on top of diced onion, pomegranate seeds, and diced beet.
3. Rub roast with olive oil, paprika, salt and pepper, and rosemary.
4. Mix together red wine, pomegranate juice, honey, and mustard, and pour over roast.
5. Cover and bake for 2-2½ hours, depending on how rare or well done you prefer.

pistachio mint crusted rack of lamb

INGREDIENTS

- 2 racks of lamb (8-bone each), trimmed and frenched
- kosher salt and black pepper
- 3 tbsp. olive oil, divided
- ½ cup pistachios, shelled, roasted, salted
- 3 cups mint leaves, loosely packed
- 3 garlic cloves, minced
- zest and juice of 1 lemon

DIRECTIONS

Note: If you don't have a large enough skillet, place a roasting pan in the oven to heat up as the oven does.

1. Preheat oven to 450°.
2. Heat an ovenproof skillet large enough to hold both racks of lamb until hot over medium-high heat.
3. Season the lamb generously with salt and pepper on all sides.
4. Heat 1 tbsp. of oil in the pan and sear the lamb on all sides for about 2 minutes per side. Let the lamb cool a little.
5. Put the pistachios in a food processor and pulse a few times to grind them. Add the remaining 2 tbsp. of olive oil, mint, garlic, zest and juice of the lemon. Process until it turns into a paste.
6. Spread the paste on the meat-side of the lamb racks, pressing down firmly. Place the lamb racks back in the skillet (or in roasting pan), bone-side down, then place pan in oven.
7. Roast for 20 minutes for medium rare, 25 minutes for medium. Cover the lamb with a piece of foil and let sit for 10 minutes before cutting the lamb into chops. Use a sharp, thin knife to carve.

cranberry corned beef

INGREDIENTS

- 1 corned beef with spices, about 4 lbs.
- 1 can cranberry sauce
- 1 tbsp. honey
- 1 tbsp. imitation mustard
- ¼ cup red wine
- 1 onion, chopped

DIRECTIONS

1. Place the corned beef with spices, fat side up, in a large stockpot.
2. Cover the beef with water and bring to a simmer. Cover and continue to simmer over low heat until the beef is fork tender, about 3-3½ hours. (Tip: The beef can be prepared the day before by marinating the meat in the liquid. Bring to a simmer the next day and proceed with the recipe.)
3. Position oven rack to top third of the oven. Preheat the broiler to low. Line a rimmed baking sheet with foil, top with a rack, and spray with non-stick cooking spray.
4. Transfer the cooked beef to the prepared rack, fat side up. Using a sharp knife, trim the fat.
5. In a small saucepan, whisk the remaining ingredients and bring to a boil over medium-high heat. Continue to boil until the mixture has slightly reduced and thickened, about 7-10 minutes. Spoon the glaze evenly over the beef.
6. Spread chopped onion over the beef, then place under the broiler and cook until the glaze has darkened and started to caramelize, about 5-10 minutes depending on how hot your broiler is. Watch carefully as you do not want the glaze to burn.
7. Remove from the oven and allow the meat to cool for 15 minutes before slicing.

sweet 'n' tangy brisket

INGREDIENTS

- 5-lb. brisket
- ½ cup ketchup
- ¼ cup imitation soy sauce (I use Glick's)
- ½ cup honey
- salt, pepper, and paprika to taste
- 1 large onion, diced

DIRECTIONS

1. Preheat oven to 400°.
2. Spread diced onion on bottom of an extra large roasting pan, then place brisket on top of the onions.
3. Rub brisket with paprika, salt and pepper.
4. Mix together ketchup, soy sauce, and honey, and pour over meat.
5. Cover and bake for 2-2½ hours depending on how rare or well done you prefer.

beef & broccoli

INGREDIENTS

- 3½ cups broccoli florets, stems removed
- 1 bell pepper (or ⅓ each of red, orange and yellow bell peppers), cut into chunks
- 1 yellow onion, diced
- 1 whole head of garlic, minced
- 1 lb. beef chunks
- 3 tbsp. vegetable oil
- 6 tbsp. imitation soy sauce (I use Glick's)
- ¼ cup Hadar orange glaze
- salt and pepper to taste

Tip: Chicken can be substituted. This recipe is excellent with leftover schnitzel!

DIRECTIONS

1. In a large wok or skillet, sauté chopped onions and garlic in vegetable oil.
2. When onions are browned, add broccoli, peppers, meat, soy sauce, orange glaze, salt and pepper.
3. Let cook over medium flame for 15 minutes or until meat is cooked through.

meatballs & "spaghetti"

INGREDIENTS

- 2 lbs. ground beef
- 3 eggs
- 1 tbsp. ketchup
- 3 tbsp. matzo meal or ground walnut
- salt and pepper
- pinch of garlic powder
- 1 tsp. parsley
- 4 cups tomato sauce
- 1 large spaghetti squash, cut in half

DIRECTIONS

1. Preheat oven to 400°.
2. Mix ground beef, eggs, ketchup, matzo meal, salt and pepper, garlic powder, and parsley.
3. Bring tomato sauce to a boil in a large pot.
4. Form meatballs and add to sauce.
5. Cook on medium flame, uncovered for 30 minutes.
6. While the meatballs are cooking, put spaghetti squash in the oven for 1 hour, or until soft.
7. Remove squash from the oven and shred the meaty part into a bowl.
8. Serve meatballs with the spaghetti squash.

Note: For fresh tomato sauce recipe, see book introduction. Or use store bought!

ROME, ITALY

Hint: For a low-cal version, you can bake (with or without matzo meal)!

eggplant lasagna

INGREDIENTS

- 2 cups tomato sauce
- 1 large eggplant,
  sliced into ½-inch thick, round pieces
- 2 eggs
- 1 cup matzo meal or ground walnut (or half and half)
- 1 lb. ground beef
- 1 large onion, diced
- salt and pepper

DIRECTIONS

1. Preheat oven to 350°.
2. Salt eggplant on both sides and leave for 30 minutes until liquid is released.
3. Dip slices of eggplant first in eggs, then in matzo meal and/or ground walnuts, seasoned with salt and pepper.
4. Fry each slice in canola oil for 2 minutes on each side until soft.
5. Brown onion and ground beef.
6. Create layers with eggplant, ground beef, and tomato sauce (creates about 3 layers).
7. Bake uncovered for 30 minutes.

SEDONA, ARIZONA

southwestern sweet 'n' spicy meatballs

INGREDIENTS

- 3 lbs. ground beef
- 3 eggs
- 1 tbsp. ketchup
- 2 tsp. lemon juice
- 3 tbsp. matzo meal or ground walnut
- 1 tbsp. parsley

Sauce:
- 16 oz. salsa (mild or spicy, depending on your preference)
- 12 oz. dark fruit jam (grape, blueberry, or black currant)
- ¼ cup ketchup
- 1 cup water
- ¼ cup sugar
- salt and pepper

DIRECTIONS

1. Mix together sauce ingredients and boil in a large pot.
2. Combine meatball ingredients and form into meatballs. Add to boiling sauce.
3. Cook on medium flame uncovered for 35 minutes.

poultry

strawberry glazed chicken

INGREDIENTS

- 2 cups strawberry preserves
- ½ cup imitation mustard
- ½ cup maple syrup or honey
- ¼ tsp. garlic powder
- 1 tsp. lemon juice
- 2 lbs. chicken breasts, cut into chunks
- ½ cup canola oil
- salt and pepper

DIRECTIONS

1. In a large bowl, whisk together the strawberry preserves, mustard, honey, garlic powder, and lemon juice, until blended.
2. In a separate bowl, mix chicken chunks with oil, salt and pepper.
3. Spray a large wok with cooking spray and heat for a minute on high flame.
4. Add chicken chunks and cook on medium flame for 10 minutes until chicken is cooked through.
5. In a separate pot, heat strawberry mixture until boiling.
6. When chicken is cooked, pour hot glaze over chicken and mix until covered.

Tip: This glaze is also great on salmon and meat!

pesto chicken "pasta"

INGREDIENTS

- 4 large chicken breasts, cut into 1-inch thick strips
- 2 cups spaghetti squash, shredded
- 1 cup walnut pesto (for recipe, see introduction)
- ½ cup sun-dried tomatoes
- 1 bell pepper, cut into thin strips (optional)
- salt and pepper

DIRECTIONS

1. Marinate chicken in pesto for about 30 minutes.
2. Sauté chicken strips in pan on medium flame until chicken is cooked through (about 7-10 minutes).
3. Add spaghetti squash, sun-dried tomatoes, and red bell pepper.
4. Season with salt and pepper, mix, and serve.

Hint: This dish can be served hot or cold, if you like more of a "pasta salad" effect!

honey glazed turkey roast

INGREDIENTS

- 5-lb. turkey roast
- 3 tbsp. olive oil
- 2 tbsp. imitation honey mustard
- 3 tbsp. orange juice
- paprika
- salt and pepper

Honey Mustard Glaze:
- 5 tbsp. mayonnaise
- 3 tbsp. imitation honey mustard
- 2 tbsp. olive oil
- 1 tsp. chopped parsley

Tip: Use leftover turkey in a chef salad!

DIRECTIONS

1. Preheat oven to 400°.
2. Rub down turkey roast with olive oil, paprika, salt and pepper.
3. Add honey mustard and orange juice, and continue massaging.
4. Cover and bake for 1½ hours.
5. While the turkey is baking, mix glaze ingredients in a bowl.
6. Drip honey mustard glaze over the turkey immediately after removing from the oven. Serve hot.

CINQUE TERRE, ITALY

lemon zested asparagus chicken

INGREDIENTS

- 1 medium lemon
- 3 tbsp. olive oil
- 1 large red onion, thinly sliced
- 1 medium garlic clove, crushed
- 6 boneless, skinless chicken breasts, trimmed and cut into ½-inch strips
- 8 cherry tomatoes, halved
- 6 medium asparagus spears, ends trimmed, cut into 2-inch pieces
- ¾ tsp. ground cumin
- ¼ cup chopped parsley
- salt and pepper to taste

DIRECTIONS

1. Finely grate 1 tsp. zest from the lemon, and juice the lemon. Set aside.
2. In a large skillet, brown onions and garlic on high flame (about 3-5 minutes).
3. Add chicken, asparagus, tomatoes, cumin, salt and pepper, and cook for 6 minutes, until chicken is cooked through.
4. Turn off the flame and add lemon juice, lemon zest, and parsley. Mix.

moroccan chicken

INGREDIENTS

- 1 whole chicken cut into 8 pieces, or 8 chicken leg quarters
- ¼ cup dried apricots
- 2 cups olives (black, green or mixed)
- ¼ cup dried figs
- 2 cups whole pearl onions or 1 large onion, diced
- ¼ cup dried dates
- 1 tsp. cinnamon
- 1 tsp. turmeric
- 1 tsp. cumin
- paprika, salt, pepper and garlic powder to taste
- 2 tbsp. honey
- 2 tbsp. olive oil

DIRECTIONS

1. Make a rub for the chicken with cinnamon, turmeric, cumin, paprika, salt, pepper, and garlic powder.
2. Preheat oven to 400° and place chicken in 10×13-inch pan, skin up, and cover with apricots, olives, figs, dates, and onion.
3. Drizzle honey and olive oil over the chicken.
4. Cover and bake for 1½ hours (for leg quarters, bake for 1 hour).

duck a l'orange

INGREDIENTS

- 1 whole 5-lb. duckling
- 1 bottle (16 oz.) orange preserves with orange zest, or zest from 1 orange
- ¼ cup white wine
- ¼ cup balsamic vinegar
- 1 onion, chopped
- 1 tbsp. olive oil
- paprika, salt, and pepper to season

DIRECTIONS

1. Preheat oven to 400°.
2. Mix together preserves, wine, and balsamic vinegar.
3. Season duck with paprika, salt, and pepper, then place, skin side up, in a sprayed 9×12-inch pan, then drizzle with olive oil.
4. Pour sauce over duck.
5. Sprinkle with chopped onion.
6. Bake at 400° for 1 hour covered, then uncover and bake for an additional 30 minutes.

baked chicken with fennel & carrots

INGREDIENTS

- ½ cup apple juice
- 2 tbsp. imitation mustard
- 1 tbsp. tarragon
- 1 tbsp. parsley, chopped
- 2 medium carrots, peeled and sliced
- 1 large yellow onion, diced

- 1 small fennel bulb, trimmed, quartered, and cut lengthwise through the core into ½-inch thick wedges
- 1 large chicken, cut into eighths
- ½ cup chicken broth
- 1 tsp. cider vinegar
- 2 large Granny Smith apples, unpeeled and diced
- salt and pepper

DIRECTIONS

1. Preheat oven to 400°.
2. Mix apple juice, mustard, broth, vinegar, salt and pepper to create dressing.
3. Scatter carrots, fennel, onions, and apples over the bottom of a 10×15-inch baking dish. Arrange the chicken pieces, skin side up, on top of vegetables.
4. Pour dressing and herbs over chicken to cover.
5. Cover and bake chicken for 1½ hours.

NEGRIL, JAMAICA

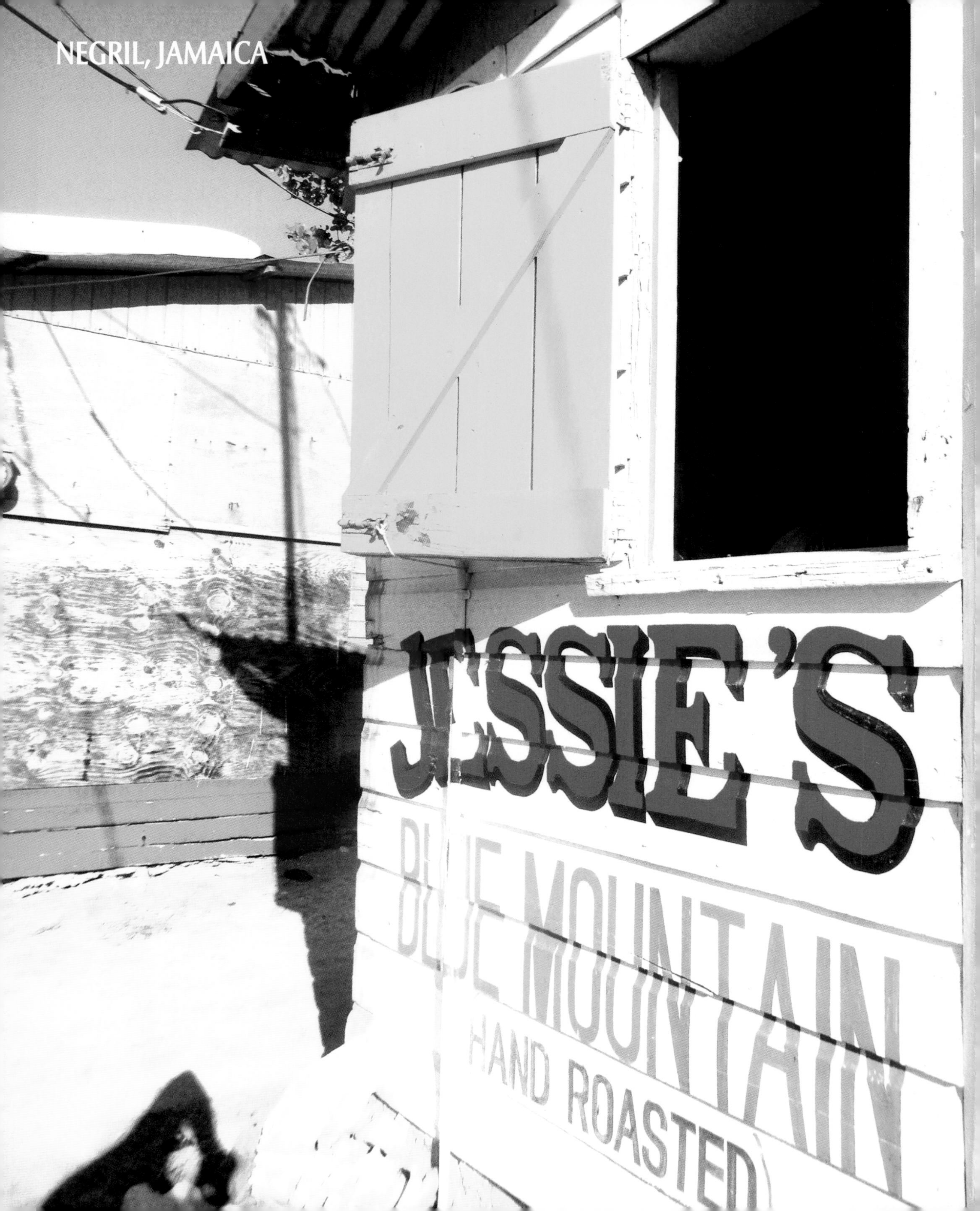

jamaican jerk chicken

INGREDIENTS

- 3 lbs. chicken thighs
- 6 jalapeño peppers, diced
- 2 tbsp. thyme
- 2 tbsp. ground cinnamon
- 8 garlic cloves, finely chopped
- 3 medium onions, finely chopped
- 2 tbsp. sugar

- 2 tbsp. salt
- 2 tsp. ground black pepper
- ½ cup olive oil
- ½ cup imitation soy sauce
- juice of one lime
- 1 cup orange juice
- 1 cup white vinegar

DIRECTIONS

1. Blend all ingredients besides chicken.
2. Marinate chicken in sauce overnight.
3. Bake chicken in the oven, covered, for 30 minutes at 400°.
4. Remove chicken from the oven and finish cooking it on a barbeque or in the broiler, allowing the chicken to get crisp and brown. Make sure to keep the chicken moist by basting occasionally.

coq au vin with saffron quinoa

INGREDIENTS

- 1 cup dry quinoa
- ½ cup dry white wine
- ½ cup water
- pinch of saffron
- ½ cup mushrooms, thinly sliced
- 4 chicken leg quarters
- 3 tbsp. olive oil
- salt and pepper
- paprika

DIRECTIONS

1. Preheat oven to 400°.
2. Pour quinoa into a 9×13-inch pan.
3. Season with salt, pepper and saffron.
4. Pour water on top of quinoa and stir.
5. Sprinkle mushrooms on top on quinoa.
6. Rub chicken with paprika, salt, pepper, and olive oil, place over quinoa in the pan.
7. Pour wine on top of chicken.
8. Cover and bake for 1 hour, then uncover and bake for an additional 15 minutes (or until chicken is cooked through).

citrus chicken

INGREDIENTS

- 1 lime, quartered
- 1 lemon, quartered
- 1 navel orange, cut into eighths
- ¼ cup orange juice
- 1 cup apricot preserves
- 1 tbsp. imitation mustard
- 1 tbsp. honey
- 1 tsp. dried or fresh dill
- 1 whole chicken, cut into eighths

DIRECTIONS

1. Preheat oven to 400°.
2. Mix orange juice, apricot preserves, mustard, honey, and dill in a bowl.
3. Spread lime, lemon, and orange on bottom of a 9×12-inch pan.
4. Place chicken on top of citrus, skin side up.
5. Pour sauce over chicken, to cover.
6. Cover and bake chicken for 1½ hours.

NEGRIL, JAMAICA

coconut crusted chicken with plum dipping sauce

INGREDIENTS

- 1 lb. chicken tenderloins or chicken breasts, sliced into long, 1-inch thick strips
- ½ cup matzo cake meal
- 2 eggs
- 1½ cups sweetened coconut, shredded
- 6 tbsp. canola oil

Plum Dipping Sauce:
- 5 ripe plums, diced
- 3 tbsp. lime juice
- ¼ cup sugar
- 1 tsp. cinnamon
- 1 tsp. cardamom

DIRECTIONS

1. Beat eggs and put aside.
2. In a separate bowl, combine cake meal and shredded coconut.
3. Dip chicken in egg mixture and then cover in coconut crumbs.
4. Fry in oil, approximately 3 minutes per side (depending on thickness of chicken), until golden brown.
5. In a small saucepan, combine plums, lime juice, and sugar and bring to a boil. Then, cook for 10-15 minutes until plums soften.
6. Let cool and add cardamom and cinnamon.
7. Serve chicken with plum dipping sauce at room temperature.

honey mustard schnitzel

INGREDIENTS

- 4 large chicken breasts, thinned out
- 1 cup matzo meal or ground walnuts
- 3 eggs
- 1 tbsp. onion soup mix

- 1 tbsp. imitation mustard
- 2 tbsp. honey
- salt and pepper
- 1 tbsp. parsley flakes

DIRECTIONS

1. Beat eggs.
2. Add onion soup mix, honey, and mustard.
3. In a separate dish, season matzo meal with salt, pepper and parsley flakes.
4. Dip chicken in egg mixture and then cover in matzo meal.
5. Fry breaded chicken breasts in oil, 3 minutes on each side (depending on thickness of chicken), or until golden brown.

VIENNA, AUSTRIA

grilled chicken with spicy mango salsa

INGREDIENTS

- 1 lb. chicken breasts
- 2 tbsp. olive oil
- 2 tbsp. honey
- 1 tsp. salt
- 1½ tsp. paprika
- ⅛ tsp. garlic powder
- ⅛ tsp. onion powder
- 2 tsp. cumin
- 2 tsp. rosemary
- salt and pepper to taste

Salsa:
- 3 mangos, diced
- juice of 2 limes
- ¼ cup cilantro, chopped
- 4 scallions, diced
- 1 tsp. cumin
- ½ tsp. garlic
- pinch of salt and pepper
- ½ small jalapeño, minced
  (with seeds and ribs removed),
  or ½ tsp. cayenne pepper

DIRECTIONS

1. In a large bowl, combine honey, salt and all spices for the chicken.
2. Coat chicken breasts lightly in olive oil, about 1 tbsp. for each breast. Rub spice mixture onto both sides of chicken breasts and return chicken to bowl.
3. Refrigerate chicken for at least 30 minutes to absorb flavors.
4. While the chicken is marinating, prepare the salsa by mixing all ingredients in a bowl.
5. To cook the chicken, you can grill it on high heat for about 15 minutes, flipping frequently; or, you can pan-fry it on medium heat for about 5 minutes per side.
6. Let chicken sit for 1-2 minutes so juices can redistribute. Serve warm with salsa.

lavender mint roasted chicken

INGREDIENTS

- One 3-lb. whole chicken
- 2 tbsp. honey
- 2 tbsp. olive oil
- salt and pepper
- paprika
- 2 tbsp. mint
- 2 tbsp. lavender
- ¼ cup white wine

DIRECTIONS

1. Preheat oven to 400°.
2. Place chicken in a large roasting tin on top of diced onions.
3. Rub chicken with olive oil, wine, honey, spices, and herbs.
4. Cover and bake for 1½ hours.

chicken with apricot marmalade & balsamic vinaigrette

INGREDIENTS

- 1 whole chicken, cut into eighths
- 1 bottle (16 oz.) apricot marmalade
  (If apricot marmalade is unavailable, you can substitute apricot jam and ¼ cup orange juice)
- ¼ cup balsamic vinegar
- 1 onion, chopped
- paprika
- salt and pepper

DIRECTIONS

1. Preheat oven to 400°.
2. Mix apricot marmalade and balsamic vinegar in a bowl.
3. Rub chicken with paprika, salt and pepper, and lay in a sprayed 9×12-inch pan, skin side up.
4. Pour apricot and balsamic sauce over chicken.
5. Sprinkle chopped onion over the chicken.
6. Cover and bake for 1 hour, then uncover the chicken and bake for another 15 minutes.

mediterranean chicken

INGREDIENTS

- 1 whole chicken cut into 8 pieces, or 8 chicken leg quarters
- 2 cups sun-dried tomatoes
- 2 cups olives (black, green or mixed)
- 2 cups marinated artichokes
- 2 cups whole pearl onions or 1 large onion, diced
- 1 tbsp. za'atar
- paprika
- salt and pepper
- garlic powder
- 1 tbsp. lemon juice
- 1 tbsp. olive oil

DIRECTIONS

1. Preheat oven to 400°.
2. Rub the chicken with za'atar, paprika, garlic powder, salt and pepper.
3. Place chicken in 10×13-inch pan, skin up, and cover with sun-dried tomatoes, olives, artichokes, and onions.
4. Drizzle lemon juice and olive oil over the chicken.
5. Cover and bake for 1½ hours (for leg quarters, bake for only 1 hour).

dairy & pareve entrees

"pasta" primavera

INGREDIENTS

- 1 small spaghetti squash (about 4 cups), baked, seeded and shredded
- 1 onion, diced
- 2-3 tbsp. garlic, minced
- 20 oz. spinach leaves
- 1 cup sun-dried tomatoes
- 1 package ricotta cheese (16 oz.)
- 3 tbsp. Parmesan cheese
- ¼ cup olive oil
- salt and pepper

DIRECTIONS

1. Sauté the onion and garlic in olive oil until brown.
2. Add sun-dried tomatoes and spinach.
3. Add ricotta cheese, Parmesan, salt and pepper.
4. Continue to cook over flame for 2 minutes.
5. Mix all ingredients with the cooked and shredded spaghetti squash.
6. Sprinkle extra Parmesan cheese over the dish before serving.

BURANO, ITALY

baked "ziti"

INGREDIENTS

- 1 small spaghetti squash,
  (about 4 cups), baked, seeded and shredded
- 1 onion, diced
- 2 cups tomato sauce
  (recipe in book intro)
- 1 package ricotta cheese (16 oz.)
- 16 oz. shredded mozzarella cheese
- 3 tbsp. Parmesan cheese
- salt and pepper to taste

DIRECTIONS

1. Preheat oven to 400°.
2. Mix all ingredients together.
3. Spread mixture in a greased 9×12-inch baking dish.
4. Bake, uncovered, for 30 minutes or until cheese is melted desired amount. If you prefer the cheese to be browned, this will need a little more time in the oven.

mint & honey baked salmon

INGREDIENTS

- 4 salmon fillets (6 oz. each)
- 2 tsp. mint
- 1 tsp. basil
- 1 tsp. dill

- 2 tbsp. lemon juice
- 2 tbsp. honey
- ¼ cup white wine
- 1 tsp. paprika
- salt and pepper

DIRECTIONS

1. Preheat the oven to 400°.
2. Pat the salmon fillet dry with paper towel and sprinkle salt on the skin side. Place salmon on a baking tray, skin side down.
3. In a small bowl, combine all ingredients (except salmon). Mix well. Smear the marinade over the fish fillets.
4. Place fish in the oven for 10-15 minutes, depending on the thickness of the fish.
5. Once the internal temperature of the salmon reaches 120 degrees, remove it from the oven and serve immediately with a fresh squeeze of lemon juice.

SIPAN, CROATIA

salmon croquettes with wild mushroom sauce

INGREDIENTS

- 2 cans filleted salmon, flaked
- 1 egg, beaten
- 2 tbsp. green onions, diced
- ½ cup matzo meal
- vegetable oil, for frying

Wild Mushroom Sauce:
- 1 tbsp. unsalted butter
- extra virgin olive oil
- 2 shallots, minced
- 2 lbs. assorted mushrooms, such as crimini, oyster, shiitake, chanterelle, or white, trimmed and sliced
- leaves from 2 fresh thyme sprigs
- salt and pepper
- ½ cup cabernet sauvignon
- ¼ cup low-sodium vegetable broth
- ¼ cup heavy cream
- 1 tbsp. fresh chives, minced

DIRECTIONS

Salmon Croquettes:

1. Combine canned salmon, beaten egg, green onions, and ¼ cup matzo meal. Form into patties and dust with additional matzo meal.
2. Over medium heat, heat oil in a medium skillet. Fry salmon croquettes until golden brown, about 2 minutes on each side.

Mushroom Sauce:

1. Heat butter and a splash of oil in a skillet over medium heat. When the butter starts to foam add the shallots and sauté for 2 minutes to soften.
2. Add the mushrooms and thyme; season with salt and pepper. Stir everything together for a few minutes.
3. Add the red wine, stirring to scrape up any stuck bits, then cook and stir to evaporate the alcohol. When the wine is almost all gone, add the vegetable broth. Let the liquid cook down and then remove from the heat.
4. Stir in the cream and chives and season with salt and pepper.

moroccan baked salmon

INGREDIENTS

- 6 salmon fillets (about 6 oz. each)
- ½ red bell pepper, diced
- ½ yellow bell pepper, diced
- ½ orange bell pepper, diced
- 1 onion, diced
- ½ cup pitted green olives
- 2 tsp. cumin
- 5 tbsp. olive oil
- salt and pepper

DIRECTIONS

1. Sauté onions and peppers in olive oil for 5 minutes.
2. Preheat oven to 350°.
3. Place salmon in a 9×12-inch pan and season with spices.
4. Pour sautéed peppers, olives, and onions on top of seasoned salmon.
5. Cover and bake for 30 minutes or until salmon is cooked through.

rosemary walnut crusted salmon with garlic aioli

INGREDIENTS

- 2 cups ground walnuts
- ½ cup matzo meal
- salt and pepper
- 1 tbsp. dried rosemary
- 2 eggs
- 6 salmon fillets (about 6 oz. each)
- lemon juice

Garlic Aioli:
- ½ cup mayonnaise
- 2 garlic cloves, minced
- 1 tbsp. lemon juice
- ½ tsp. imitation mustard
- salt

DIRECTIONS

1. Pour lemon juice over salmon fillets.
2. Beat eggs in a bowl, and dip salmon fillets in egg.
3. In a separate bowl or pan, mix walnuts, matzo meal, rosemary, salt and pepper, and then coat salmon in this mixture.
4. Fry salmon on medium heat for 5-6 minutes per side for thick fillets, or 2-3 minutes per side for thinner fillets.
5. Mix all ingredients for garlic aioli in a bowl, then serve salmon with garlic aioli on the side.

tuscan tuna steak with mint yogurt sauce

INGREDIENTS

- 1½ lbs. fresh tuna steaks, 1 inch thick
- 2 tbsp. black pepper
- pinch of cayenne pepper
- 2 tsp. paprika
- 2 tbsp. olive oil
- 2 tbsp. butter

Mint Yogurt Sauce:
- 1 cup plain yogurt
- 1 tbsp. garlic powder or chopped fresh garlic
- ½ cup chopped mint
- 1 tsp. lime or lemon juice
- pinch of salt

DIRECTIONS

1. Generously coat tuna with black pepper and cayenne pepper.
2. Heat oil and butter in a large skillet over high heat. When oil is nearly smoking, place steaks in pan. Cook on one side for 3-4 minutes, or until blackened. Turn steaks, and cook for additional 3-4 minutes, or to desired doneness.
3. In a small mixing bowl, combine all yogurt sauce ingredients. Stir well. Refrigerate until ready to use, then serve with tuna, on the side.

BURANO, ITALY

honey mustard poached salmon

INGREDIENTS

- 6 salmon fillets
- 1 large onion, diced
- 1 tbsp. dill
- 2 tbsp. lemon juice
- ¼ cup orange juice
- ¼ cup imitation honey mustard
- salt and pepper
- paprika

DIRECTIONS

1. Brown onion in a large skillet.
2. Mix salt, pepper, and paprika in a bowl.
3. Rub salmon with spice mixture.
4. Add salmon to skillet with dill, lemon juice, orange juice, and honey mustard.
5. Cover and cook on low flame for 20 minutes, or until salmon is cooked through.

fresh sea bass with grapefruit relish

INGREDIENTS

- 2 ruby or pink grapefruits
- 1 navel orange
- 1 tbsp. fresh cilantro, chopped
- 1 tbsp. fresh mint, chopped
- 4½ lbs. fresh sea bass, skin and pin bones removed
- salt and pepper to taste
- 1 tbsp. olive oil, plus additional for drizzling

DIRECTIONS

1. Peel, segment and dice the grapefruits, letting the segments and any juices fall into a bowl. Add mint and cilantro and stir gently.
2. Season the sea bass fillets with salt and pepper. In a heavy frying pan over medium-high heat, warm the olive oil. Add the seasoned sea bass and cook until browned underneath, 3-4 minutes. Turn the sea bass over and cook until opaque around the edges, about 3 minutes more.
3. Transfer the sea bass to individual plates. Spoon the grapefruit-mint mixture on top and drizzle with a little olive oil. Serve immediately.

eggplant parmigiana

INGREDIENTS

- 2 cups tomato sauce
- 1 large eggplant,
  sliced into ½-inch thick, round pieces
- 2 eggs
- 1 cup matzoh meal or ground walnut
  (or half & half)

- 8 oz. mozzarella cheese
- 3 oz. goat cheese
  (if unavailable, substitute
  with additional mozzarella)
- salt and pepper

DIRECTIONS

1. Preheat oven to 350°.
2. Salt eggplant on both sides and leave for 30 minutes until liquid is released.
3. Crack and mix eggs in one bowl, and pour matzo meal and/or ground walnuts and seasoning into a second bowl.
4. Dip eggplant slices first in eggs, then in matzo meal and/or ground walnuts.
5. Fry each slice in canola oil for 2 minutes on each side until soft.
6. In a 9×12-inch pan, create layers with eggplant, goat cheese, and tomato sauce (creates about 3 layers).
7. Top with mozzarella cheese.
8. Bake uncovered for 20 minutes or until mozzarella cheese is melted.

Tip: For a low-cal version, leave out the matzo meal and/or frying and just bake!

desserts

carrot muffins

INGREDIENTS

- 1 box Manischewitz extra moist yellow cake mix
- 1 large egg
- ½ cup cold water or almond milk
- 3 tbsp. vegetable oil

- 2 jars carrot baby food
- 1 tsp. cinnamon
- 1 tsp. vanilla extract
- chopped walnuts or crumbled macaroons with 1 tsp. cinnamon

DIRECTIONS

1. Preheat oven to 350°.
2. Grease a 9×12-inch muffin tin.
3. Empty cake mix into a large mixing bowl.
4. Add water, eggs, oil and baby food.
5. Beat with an electric mixer on medium speed for 4 minutes.
6. Distribute batter evenly into muffin tin.
7. Top muffins with chopped walnuts or crumbled macaroons with cinnamon.
8. Bake uncovered for 1 hour or until toothpick inserted in center comes out clean.
9. Let cool for 15 minutes.

apple cranberry crunch

INGREDIENTS

Apple/Cranberry Mixture:
- 4 large apples, diced
- 2 cans (32 oz.) cranberry sauce

Crumb Topping:
- 1 cup ground walnuts
- 1 cup matzo cake meal
- 1 cup canola oil
- 1 cup sugar

DIRECTIONS

1. Preheat oven to 350° and spray 9×12-inch pan with vegetable cooking spray.
2. Spread diced apples on the bottom of pan.
3. Cover apples with cranberry sauce.
4. Combine ingredients for crumb topping in a bowl.
5. Sprinkle crumb topping over the apple/cranberry mixture.
6. Bake at 350° uncovered for 1 hour.

banana cake

INGREDIENTS

- 2 boxes Manischewitz extra moist yellow cake mix
- 2 large eggs
- 1 cup cold water or almond milk
- 6 tbsp. vegetable oil
- 2-3 ripe bananas
- 1 tsp. cinnamon
- 1 tsp. vanilla extract
- 2 cups either ground walnuts, or crumbled macaroons with 1 tsp. cinnamon

DIRECTIONS

1. Preheat oven to 350°.
2. Grease a 9×12-inch baking pan.
3. Empty both bags of yellow cake mix into a large mixing bowl.
4. Add water (or almond milk), eggs, oil, and bananas.
5. Beat with an electric mixer on medium speed for 4 minutes.
6. Spread batter evenly in greased pan.
7. Top with chopped walnuts or crumbled macaroons with cinnamon.
8. Bake uncovered for 1 hour or until toothpick inserted in center comes out clean.
9. Let cool for 15 minutes.

viennese crunch

INGREDIENTS

- 1 cup margarine
- 1 egg
- 1 tsp. instant coffee
- 1 cup sugar

- 1 cup matzo cake meal
- ¼ tsp. salt
- 12 oz. chocolate chips
- 1 cup chopped nuts, any kind

DIRECTIONS

1. Preheat oven to 350°.
2. Put margarine in a bowl and beat on medium speed, adding sugar slowly, until the mixture has a creamy texture. Add the sugar, egg, coffee, cake meal, and salt.
3. Spread mixture onto a cookie sheet and bake for 20 minutes.
4. Remove from oven and sprinkle the chocolate chips on top, spreading them as they melt.
5. Sprinkle nuts on top of chocolate.
6. Cut into squares while warm.

coconut cream pie in a macaroon crust

INGREDIENTS

- 30 oz. non-dairy whipped topping
- 2¾ cups cold almond milk, divided
- 1 cup shredded coconut, toasted
- 2 packages (4-serving size) instant vanilla pudding
- 1½ cups crushed macaroons
- 6 tbsp. of melted butter or margarine
- ½ pint whipping cream

DIRECTIONS

1. Preheat oven to 350°.
2. Prepare the crust by mixing the macaroon crumbs together with the melted butter. Pat the macaroon and butter mixture down into a pie plate, covering the sides and bottom. Bake for 10-12 minutes. Once it is baked, set aside to cool.
3. If you haven't toasted the coconut yet, do so now. Simply place shredded coconut in a pan over low to medium heat, stirring constantly until it is browned slightly on the edges. Set aside to cool.
4. Put whipped topping mix and 1 cup of almond milk in a large bowl, then blend with an electric mixer on high speed for 6 minutes or until topping thickens and forms peaks.
5. Add remaining 1¾ cups almond milk and pudding mixes, and blend on low speed until completely combined. Then beat on high speed for 2 minutes, scraping bowl occasionally.
6. Fold in ¾ cup of the toasted coconut. Set the rest aside for the top.
7. Spoon the mixture into your baked crust.
8. Whip the whipping cream with a hand mixer until soft peaks form, approximately 5-7 minutes. Spoon over the pie filling.
9. Refrigerate for at least 4 hours. After the filling has set, sprinkle the remaining coconut on the top of your pie just before serving so it remains crisp. Serve and enjoy.

raspberry shortcake trifle

INGREDIENTS

- 3 packages Manischewitz yellow cake mix
- 6 eggs
- ¾ cup non-dairy whipped topping
- ¾ cup cold water
- 1 jar (12 oz.) raspberry or black currant jam
- 2 cups raspberries, preferably fresh
- One 8 oz. container whipped cream

DIRECTIONS

1. Preheat oven to 350°.
2. In a large bowl, mix yellow cake mix, eggs, whipped topping, and water.
3. Divide batter into three 8-inch round pans.
4. Bake for 40 minutes (or until inserted toothpick comes out clean).
5. Let cakes cool for 30 minutes.
6. Remove one cake from pan and place at the bottom of a trifle bowl.
7. Spread jam and then whipped cream.
8. Place second cake on top of jam and whipped cream layer, and repeat with the third cake.
9. Top with remaining whipped cream and raspberries.

SUGARLOAF, NEW YORK

country rustic apple pie

INGREDIENTS

Apple Mixture:
- 6 apples, peeled, cored, and sliced
- ½ cup of sugar
- ½ tsp. cinnamon
- 2 tbsp. apricot jam
- 2 tsp. lemon juice

Crumb Topping:
- ½ cup sugar
- ¾ cup cake meal
- ⅛ tsp. salt
- 6 tbsp. margarine
- ¼ cup chopped nuts (optional)

DIRECTIONS

1. Preheat oven to 350°.
2. Combine the apples, sugar, cinnamon, apricot jam, and lemon juice.
3. Pour the apple mixture into a greased 1½-quart casserole pan.
4. In a bowl, blend the ingredients for the crumb topping until the mixture has a crumbly consistency.
5. Sprinkle crumb topping mixture over the apple mixture.
6. Bake for 1 hour uncovered.

blueberry crumble

INGREDIENTS

Blueberry Filling:
- 4 cups fresh blueberries
- ¼ cup white sugar
  (do not add sugar if blueberries
  are naturally very sweet)
- juice of 1 lemon

Crust and Crumb Topping:
- ¾ cup white sugar
- ¼ cup brown sugar
- 1 tsp. baking powder
- 2 cups ground almonds
- 2 cups matzo cake meal
- ¼ tsp. salt
- zest of 1 lemon
- ¼ cup (½ stick) unsalted butter or
  margarine, cold and cut into cubes
- 1 egg
- ¼ cup toasted slivered almonds

DIRECTIONS

1. Preheat oven to 375° and grease a 9×13-inch baking pan.
2. In a mixing bowl combine the blueberry filling ingredients. Stir until mixed well and set aside.
3. In a separate bowl, mix together the white sugar, brown sugar, baking powder, ground almonds, cake meal, salt, and lemon zest until well combined. Add the butter and egg, and use a pastry cutter to blend the ingredients until well combined and you still have pea-sized chunks of butter. Mix in the slivered almonds.
4. Place half of the crust mixture into the baking dish and press it firmly into the bottom. Spoon the blueberry mixture into crust, being careful not to add too much of the liquid.
5. Crumble the rest of the crust mixture over the blueberries so that it is evenly distributed. Bake for 50 minutes until the crumb topping is golden brown.
6. Let cool for at least an hour before cutting. Cut into 24 squares. This dish is best served just slightly above room temperature, but any leftovers can be stored in the refrigerator.

hazelnut cream cookies

INGREDIENTS

- 1 cup sugar
- ½ cup salted butter or margarine, softened
- ⅔ cup almond milk
- 1½ cup ground hazelnuts

- 1 egg
- 1 tsp. vanilla extract
- 2½ tsp. baking powder
- ¼ tsp. salt
- 1 tsp. lemon juice
- chocolate spread ("Hashachar Ha'ole" brand)

DIRECTIONS

1. Preheat oven to 350º.
2. Combine sugar and butter in a large bowl. Beat at medium speed, scraping bowl often, until creamy.
3. Add almond milk, egg, and vanilla extract. Continue beating until well mixed. Reduce speed to low, then add ground hazelnuts, baking powder, and salt. Beat, scraping bowl often, until well mixed.
4. Drop dough by rounded teaspoonfuls, 2 inches apart, onto ungreased cookie sheets. Make a welt in the middle of the cookie with your finger.
5. Bake 10-12 minutes or until lightly browned. Fill with chocolate spread when cool.

no-bake chocolate mousse pie

INGREDIENTS

- 10 chocolate chip macaroons
- 1 tbsp. butter, melted
- 6 oz. semi-sweet chocolate chips
- ¼ cup water
- ¼ cup white sugar
- 2 eggs
- One 7 oz. can whipped cream

DIRECTIONS

1. Crumble the macaroons in a medium-size mixing bowl. Combine the macaroon crumbles with the melted butter or margarine. Press mixture with your hands into a 9-inch pie plate.
2. Melt chocolate chips in a double boiler. Stir occasionally until smooth. Pour water into the chocolate and continue stirring until blended. Remove the chocolate from the heat.
3. Whip the sugar and eggs until thick and pale. Fold the chocolate mixture into the bowl with the sugar and eggs. Fold half of the whipped cream into the mixture.
4. Pour mixture into the pie crust. Decorate with remaining cream.

chocolate chip biscotti

INGREDIENTS

- 2 cups sugar
- 2 sticks margarine
- 6 large eggs
- 2¾ cups matzo cake meal
- ¾ cup potato starch
- ½ tsp. fine sea salt
- 1 cup walnuts, chopped finely
- 2 cups semi-sweet chocolate chips

Topping:
- 2 tsp. sugar
- 1 tsp. cinnamon

DIRECTIONS

1. Preheat oven to 350°.
2. Cover 2 cookie sheets with parchment paper.
3. In a mixing bowl, cream the sugar and margarine with an electric mixer on medium speed. Beat until light and fluffy approximately 5 minutes.
4. Add the eggs one at a time and continue beating.
5. In a medium bowl, whisk together the matzo cake meal, potato starch, salt and walnuts.
6. Add walnut mixture to the egg mixture in 3 sections, stirring between additions. Stir in the chocolate chips by hand.
7. Divide the dough in half and place it on the cookie sheets. Dampen your hands and shape each half in a 7×11-inch rectangle.
8. In a small bowl, combine sugar and cinnamon. Sprinkle evenly on both loaves.
9. Bake for 45 minutes to an hour, or until golden brown.
10. Remove from oven and let cool. Cut into slices diagonally, while the biscotti are still warm.
11. Cool completely before serving.

kids' favorite chocolate chip cupcakes

INGREDIENTS

- 2 boxes Manischewitz extra moist yellow cake mix or
  2 boxes Gefen extra moist cake mix
- 2 large eggs
- 1 cup cold water
- 6 tbsp. vegetable oil

- 1 package (9 oz.) chocolate chips
- chocolate spread
  (I use "Hashachar Ha'ole" brand)

DIRECTIONS

1. Preheat oven to 350°.
2. Grease 9×12-inch baking pan.
3. Empty both bags of cake mix into a large mixing bowl.
4. Add water, eggs, and oil.
5. Beat with an electric mixer on medium speed for 4 minutes.
6. Spread batter evenly in greased pan.
7. Sprinkle chocolate chips in an even layer on top of the batter.
8. Bake for 1 hour or until toothpick inserted in center comes out clean.
9. Let cake cool for 15 minutes.
10. Frost with chocolate spread.

Tip: This recipe works great as cupcakes or cake!

apple cranberry crunch: 145
apple pie, country rustic: 153
au gratin, cauliflower: 55
banana cake: 146
barbeque: 103
beef & broccoli: 83
beef goulash, hungarian: 75
beef salad, thai asian: 31
beet salad, golden ruby: 16
biscotti, chocolate chip: 159
blueberry crumble: 154
bok choy with garlic & ginger: 69
brisket, pomegranate: 78
brisket, sweet 'n' tangy: 82
broccoli, beef: 83
broccoli soup with chives: 35
brussels sprouts, garlic: 48
butternut squash, rosemary: 57
butternut squash soup, roasted: 39
cabbage & quinoa: 44
cabbage soup with matzo meatballs: 38
carrot fries, cajun: 47
carrot muffins: 142
carrots, mint & honey glazed: 58
casserole: 153
cauliflower au gratin: 55
cauliflower soup: 37
cauliflower, tri-color: 51
cheeses
    feta: 15, 28
    mozzarella: 123, 138
    parmesan: xi, 120, 123
    ricotta: 61, 120, 123
chef salad, traditional: 14
chicken
    baked chicken w. fennel & carrots: 101
    chicken breast: 27, 92, 94, 97, 109–110, 113
    chicken tenderloins: 109
    chicken w. apricot marmalade & balsamic vinaigrette: 116

citrus chicken: 107
coconut chicken w. plum sauce: 109
coq au vin with saffron quinoa: 104
grilled chicken w. spicy mango salsa: 113
honey mustard schnitzel: 110
lavender mint roasted chicken: 114
lemon zested asparagus chicken: 97
mediterranean chicken: 117
moroccan chicken: 98
pesto chicken "pasta": 94
poached peach & chicken salad: 27
strawberry glazed chicken: 92
chocolate chip biscotti: 159
chocolate mousse pie, no-bake: 157
citrus: 25, 97, 100, 107, 136
coconut cream pie in a macaroon crust: 150
cookies, hazelnut cream: 156
coq au vin with saffron quinoa: 104
corned beef: 14, 81
cranberry corned beef: 81
cranberry crunch, apple: 145
cranberry sauce: 81, 145
cream of broccoli soup with chives: 35
cream of cauliflower soup: 37
cream pie in a macaroon crust, coconut: 150
croquettes, salmon w. mushroom sauce: 127
crumble, blueberry: 154
crunch, apple cranberry: 145
cucumber salad, lemon: 25
cultural foods
    cajun: 47
    hungarian: 75
    italian: 71
    japanese: 67
    mediterranean: 117
    moroccan: 98, 128
    southwestern: 89
    spanish: 65
    thai: 31
deli: 14
desserts
    apple cranberry crunch: 145

banana cake: 146
blueberry crumble: 154
carrot muffins: 142
chocolate chip biscotti: 159
coconut cream pie, macaroon crust: 150
country rustic apple pie: 153
hazelnut cream cookies: 156
no-bake chocolate mousse pie: 157
raspberry shortcake trifle: 151
viennese crunch: 149
dips and sauces
   dips: 87, 109–110, 131, 138
   dressing: 14, 20, 24, 101
   guacamole: 19
   mint yogurt sauce: 132
   plum dipping sauce: 109
   southwestern meatball sauce: 89
   spicy mango salsa: 113
   tomato basil sauce: xi (intro)
   truffled mushroom sauce: 77
   walnut pesto: xi (intro), 94
   wild mushroom sauce: 127
duck a l'orange: 100
eggplant
   eggplant lasagna: 87
   eggplant parmigiana: 138
   grilled eggplant salad: 23
fish
   fresh sea bass w. grapefruit relish: 136
   rosemary walnut crusted salmon w. garlic aioli: 131
   salmon: 124, 127–128, 131, 135
   salmon croquettes w. wild mushroom sauce: 127
   tuscan tuna w. mint yogurt sauce: 132
flanken, roasted garlic soup: 33
fries, cajun carrot: 47
garlic brussels sprouts: 48
garlic soup with flanken, roasted: 33
garlic spaghetti squash with basil: 42
goat cheese salad, pomegranate: 28

goulash, hungarian beef: 75
grapefruit relish, fresh sea bass: 136
greek salad with mint & feta: 15
guacamole: 19
hazelnut cream cookies: 156
honey glazed turkey roast: 95
honey mustard schnitzel: 110
kugel, salt & pepper: 43
lamb, pistachio mint crusted: 80
lamb shashlik: 76
lasagna, eggplant: 87
lavender mint roasted chicken: 114
lemon cucumber salad: 25
lemon zested asparagus chicken: 97
macaroon crust, coconut cream pie: 150
macaroons: 142, 146, 150, 157
matzo meatballs, cabbage soup: 38
meat
   beef & broccoli: 83
   cranberry corned beef: 81
   eggplant lasagna: 87
   hungarian beef goulash: 75
   lamb shashlik: 76
   meatballs & "spaghetti": 84
   pistachio mint crusted rack of lamb: 80
   pomegranate brisket: 78
   southwestern sweet 'n' spicy meatballs: 89
   sweet 'n' tangy brisket: 82
   thai asian beef salad: 31
meatballs, southwestern sweet 'n' spicy: 89
meatballs & "spaghetti": 84
mint & honey glazed baby carrots: 58
mint yogurt sauce, tuscan tuna steak: 132
mousse pie, no-bake chocolate: 157
muffins, carrot: 142
mushroom salad, warm: 21
mushroom sauce, salmon croquettes: 127
mushroom spinach quinoa: 56
mushrooms, sautéed greens with portabella: 53

nuts: 80, 149, 153
pareve entrees
    fresh sea bass w. grapefruit relish: 136
    "pasta" primavera: 120
    rosemary walnut salmon w. garlic aioli: 131
    salmon croquettes w. wild mushroom sauce: 127
    tuscan tuna steak w. mint yogurt sauce: 132
parmigiana, eggplant: 138
parsnip mash: 63
parsnips, roasted: 59
"pasta," pesto chicken: 94
"pasta" primavera: 120
peach & chicken salad, poached: 27
pesto chicken "pasta": 94
pie
    coconut cream pie, macaroon crust: 150
    country rustic apple pie: 153
    no-bake chocolate mousse pie: 157
pistachio mint crusted rack of lamb: 80
plum dipping sauce, coconut chicken: 109
pomegranate brisket: 78
pomegranate & goat cheese salad: 28
portabella mushrooms, sautéed greens: 53
quinoa
    coq au vin w. saffron quinoa: 104
    mixed berry quinoa w. almonds: 68
    mushroom spinach quinoa: 56
    quinoa & cabbage: 44
    quinoa green salad: 20
    quinoa taboule: 71
    spanish quinoa: 65
raspberry shortcake trifle: 151
rosemary butternut squash: 57
salads
    chef salad: 14
    golden ruby beet salad: 16
    greek salad with mint & feta: 15

    grilled eggplant salad: 23
    heirloom tomato salad w. honey basil vinaigrette: 24
    lemon cucumber salad: 25
    poached peach & chicken salad: 27
    pomegranate & goat cheese salad: 28
    quinoa green salad: 20
    thai asian beef salad: 31
    traditional chef salad: 14
    warm mushroom salad: 21
salmon croquettes w. wild mushroom sauce: 127
salmon w. garlic aioli, rosemary walnut: 131
salt & pepper kugel: 43
schnitzel, honey mustard: 110
sea bass with grapefruit relish, fresh: 136
shashlik, lamb: 76
sides
    baby bok choy w. garlic & ginger: 69
    cajun carrot fries: 47
    cauliflower au gratin: 55
    garlic brussels sprouts: 48
    garlic spaghetti squash w. basil: 42
    mint & honey glazed baby carrots: 58
    mixed berry quinoa w. roasted almonds: 68
    mushroom spinach quinoa: 56
    parsnip mash: 63
    quinoa & cabbage: 44
    quinoa taboule: 71
    roasted parsnips: 59
    rosemary butternut squash: 57
    salt & pepper kugel: 43
    sautéed greens w. portabella mushrooms: 53
    spanish quinoa: 65
    tri-color cauliflower: 51
soups and stews
    cabbage soup with matzo meatballs: 38
    cream of broccoli soup with chives: 35
    cream of cauliflower soup: 37

hungarian beef goulash: 75
roasted butternut squash soup: 39
roasted garlic soup with flanken: 33
"spaghetti," meatballs: 84
spaghetti squash with basil, garlic: 42
spicy mango salsa, grilled chicken: 113
spinach quinoa, mushroom: 56
squash
butternut squash: 39, 57
spaghetti squash: 42–43, 84, 94, 120, 123
zucchini: 61, 67
zucchini blossoms: 61
squash soup, roasted butternut: 39
strawberry glazed chicken: 92
taboule, quinoa: 71
tomato basil sauce: xi (intro)
tomato salad with honey basil vinaigrette,
heirloom: 24
trifle, raspberry shortcake: 151
tuna steak with mint yogurt sauce, tuscan: 132
turkey roast, honey glazed: 95
viennese crunch: 149
walnut pesto: xi (intro), 94
yogurt sauce, tuscan tuna steak with mint: 132
ziti: 123

About the Author

Aviva Kanoff is an artiste extraordinaire. She is a painter, photographer and mixed media artist. As a former student of the French Culinary Institute, Aviva's artistic approach led her to creative experimentation with food.

After years of working as a personal chef, she's written her first book, *The No-Potato Passover*, combining her creativity with her intuitive understanding of flavors as well as her love of travel.